Addressing the El<

First published in Great Bri

Much Fruit Publishing

muchfruitpublishing@gmail.com

A catalogue record for this book is

available from the British Library

ISBN 978-0-9928955-4-9

Printed and bound in the United Kingdom by

R. J. Osborn Printers, Brightlingsea

Cover design by Roopop Design

Addressing the Elephant

ADDRESSING THE ELEPHANT

Contents

Addressing the Elephant

FOREWORD

I think that, once you have read this book – which I encourage you to do, urgently and carefully – you will agree that Roger has answered his own call for a prophetic voice to this generation. It gripped me from the first word, and I couldn't put it down until I had read it all the way through!

As you read it, you will hear the heart of a true pastor – a pastor with a heart for the flock, but also with a heart for the holiness of God. You cannot have a healthy church apart from the holiness of God, as unpacked in this book.

But this is no unfeeling 'writing off' of the suffering and misery caused by the Covid-19 pandemic. Roger is as much affected by all the suffering as any of us, and, I know, grieves over it like us all. But, having ministered with him for the best part of the last 20 years, in both the UK and in Africa, I also know that the failure of the Church to recognise and address the issues covered in this book causes him much grief too. A true pastor with the highest interests of the flock at the core of his being!

He has done the Church an immense service by not just "addressing the elephant" but "calling it out" and calling the Church to be the voice that God has always intended it to be in this ever-darkening world.

The Beatles chanted the refrain "Love, love, love" and it has not only been taken up by the world around us as the meaning of life but has been adopted by the Church to the exclusion of almost any other aspect of God's character. The Church seems to have forgotten that it represents our God, Who is first of all "Holy, Holy, Holy", as is pointed out in Chapter 2.

So, we have groped our way through the pandemic, just trying to survive, divided and side-tracked into unhelpful debates, while (deliberately?) ignoring the elephant in the room. That God might be active in the events of the last two years is just too terrible to contemplate. Or is it?

In the book of Jeremiah, chapter 18, God addresses His own people and says:
"If at any time I declare concerning a nation or a kingdom, that I will pluck up and break down and destroy it, and if that nation, concerning which I have spoken, turns from its evil, I will relent of the disaster that I intended to do to it. And if at any time I declare concerning a nation or a kingdom that I will build and plant it, and if it does evil in my sight, not listening to my voice, then I will relent of the good that I had intended to do to it" (ESV. verses 7-10).

In this book, Roger makes a clear case that, through this pandemic, God wants: to get the attention of the Church and this World; to show us that our Western nations and culture are ripe for His judgment; and to show us that He is looking for a response, a change of heart and direction – in a word, repentance!

The history of God's people in the Old Testament reveals that they completely ignored what the prophet Jeremiah was saying to them and replied to the Almighty:
"That is in vain! We will follow our own plans and will every one act according to the stubbornness of his evil heart" (ESV. Jeremiah chapter 18 verse 12).

They ignored what God was saying. In fact, they ended up wanting to kill the very one who warned them (it can be a dangerous thing to be a prophetic voice to God's people!) and spent 70 years in captivity in Babylon. Will we learn the lesson? Are we listening?

The apostle Paul says in 1 Corinthians chapter 10 verse 11:
"Now these things happened to them as an example, but they were written down *for our instruction*, on whom the end of the ages has come."

If we are approaching the last of the last days, as both Roger and I believe, there's an urgency to this! While the Church in the Western World has shut its eyes and its ears to what God is doing, our African brothers and sisters often see it immediately. Seeing the Western Christians running around like headless chickens, some have said, "Of course! This is the Last Days! What did you expect them to look like?" We might not yet be right at the end of the end, but this could be the start of the birth pangs that the Lord Jesus warned us about in Matthew chapter 24 verse 8. Have we heeded His warning? Are we awake? Or has our enemy stolen in and sown tares among the wheat while we have been sleeping?

Roger has issued a challenge "let the prophets stand up and speak!". Roger has stood up and has spoken – you have the results in your hand (or on screen if you are reading this electronically). The challenge is, "How will you respond?" The time is short!

Let us all take up the challenge of this book, and pray, and speak out! And turn the "elephant in the room" from a threat to a blessed and fruitful opportunity!

David Serle (Bible teacher and UK Director of Transformed International)

Christendom is awash with wrong teaching and interpretation of the grace, holiness and judgment of God. This short, easy to read appraisal of the Covid-19 pandemic from a spiritual perspective, is a great resource to help those who want to understand what the grace, holiness and judgment of God truly mean. Roger's scriptural insight makes this book a valuable tool for anyone who desires to have a deeper knowledge of and relationship with God.

Bishop Laban Mbabazi (National Overseer, Christ's Co-workers Church, Uganda)

INTRODUCTION

It's unclear exactly where the saying 'Elephant in the Room' originated. Wikipedia is quite helpful in citing a number of historical instances that trace the saying back at least as far as 1814.

Ivan Krylov, a poet and fable-teller who lived between 1769 and 1844, wrote a fable entitled 'The Inquisitive Man'. The fable relates the story of a man who visits a museum, noticing all sorts of artifacts, but failing to notice an elephant.

In 1882, Mark Twain wrote 'The Stolen White Elephant', a story which recounts the activities of a group of clumsy detectives trying to locate an elephant that was actually right on the spot, almost in front of them.

Another reference is found in the Oxford English Dictionary. Here we find the first recorded use of the phrase, as a simile, in the New York Times, June 1959: "Financing schools has become a problem about equal to having an elephant in the living room. It's so big you just can't ignore it".

Today, the expression 'Elephant in the Room' has come to mean a huge, important topic, even a controversial issue, that, although obvious and known by everyone, is never even mentioned. No-one wants to discuss the issue because it is uncomfortable to face up to it; it is potentially embarrassing, controversial and reputations can stand or fall on bringing the issue to the forefront of peoples' minds.

I want to suggest, that over the last two years, we, as Bible-believing Christians, have had an elephant in the room – the Covid-19 pandemic. At this point, it may be pointed out that surely everyone has been talking about Covid-19. In fact, we can't get away from it. This is true in the sense of its existence, its appearance, its effects on human bodies, its transmissibility, its longevity, its reaction to vaccines, but there is another angle which churches, and church leaders, have almost refused to consider: Where is God in all of this? Has God had a direct hand and purpose in allowing this pandemic to occur? Where does this pandemic fit into God's timetable for mankind? You would think that these questions would be foremost in the minds of most Christians but it appears they are not. Why is this the case? Most believers are just longing for a return to a prior normality, where we can get on with our lives, even our regular Christian activities. The scientists, social commentators and politicians have sought to answer the question 'Where does Covid-19 come from' with a mixture of fact and speculation and that appears to satisfy the minds of most enquiring Christian believers. Covid-19 is just another extremely virulent disease that occurs periodically – having sought to counter it with vaccines and lifestyle choices, we must now learn to live with it as with the common influenza virus.

In this short book, I want to attempt to demonstrate how we have wandered so far away from a Biblical understanding of God to the point where we refuse to consider or are blind-sided in considering God having any hand in such a devastating pandemic. Our gospel of grace has become so distorted to the point where, like the Covid variant, Omicron, in its rapid taking over of all other variants, grace has become the dominant teaching and understanding of God's nature, character and working in today's Church.

Introduction

CHAPTER 1 – A DISTORTION OF GRACE

To ask any student of God's Word, 'Has God changed?' or 'What are the various aspects of God's nature and character?', we would almost certainly hear the answer 'No' to the first question, and a list of God's attributes to the second including, love, holiness, patience, purity, mercy, faithfulness, truth, judgment, etc. However, I want to suggest that there is a huge disparity between what we, as Bible-believing Christians, give mental assent to, and what we are truly willing to believe and live our lives by.

As stated in the introduction to this book, "Our gospel of grace has become so distorted to the point where, like the Covid variant, Omicron, in its rapid taking over of all other variants, has become the prevalent teaching and understanding of God's nature, character and working in today's Church." Please don't misunderstand what I am saying – the subject and, indeed, experience of God's grace, His underserved favour shown to you and me, is truly wonderful. Without God's grace, we would be without all hope, lost and separated from God for all eternity. God's grace, especially demonstrated in the human birth, life, death and resurrection of His Son, Jesus, has changed everything – we can now have a relationship with our Heavenly Father for all eternity. The grace of God is truly amazing.

However, we must clear up some misconceptions about God's grace:

Firstly, His grace is but one of the many characteristics of God's nature, which all deserve a proper and full understanding and consistent teaching in today's Church. I would go so far as to say, for example, that we cannot properly understand God's grace without understanding His holiness – the cross only makes sense if we grasp that God had no choice but to pour out His holy anger on His Son, Jesus, if He was to make forgiveness available for all mankind. Sin is so abhorrent to a holy God and fully deserves His judgment – He cannot overlook or excuse even one sin, let alone the sins of billions of individuals. Those sins had to be paid for in full. The cross is truly about the meeting of God's holiness and His grace in equal measure.

Secondly, God's grace did not begin on the pages of the New Testament as if He had a complete change of heart as regards His future dealings with mankind from the time that Jesus entered this World in human flesh. The Old Testament is full of the grace of God – His undeserved favour shown to the likes of Abraham, Moses, David, and so many other Biblical figures, both those considered to be spiritual giants and those who were minnows in God's plans and purposes. To many believers today, the Old Testament portrays the holiness, anger and judgment of God more than anything else, whereas the New Testament is all about His grace, forgiveness, and eternal life, but this is such a distortion of the truth. You only need to read the Psalms to be constantly reminded of God steadfast love (lovingkindness in the KJV), His faithfulness, His mercy, His forgiveness., etc. Conversely, studying the book of Revelation, in the New Testament, reminds us that God is still very much reserving severe judgment in the future for an unbelieving World.

Thirdly, the grace of God shown to each one of us does not negate the need to live according to God's holy standards. In the epistle to the Hebrews chapter 12, verse 14, the writer, in addressing the Jewish believers in Messiah, states that there is a 'striving' or 'putting effort into' living a holy life, without which "no-one will see the Lord". This introduces the need for sanctification (lives set apart in holy living) as well as justification (declared not guilty and freed from sin) in order to enjoy the fulness of life that Jesus has won for us. The work of Jesus on the cross has opened the way for each one of us to enjoy God's forgiveness and eternal life. However, the life of God planted in us at the point of new birth contains the DNA of a holy God, which, as this life is fashioned within us, produces a character that reflects the very character of Jesus Himself. Paul refers to this as he addresses the Galatian believers, when he states, "My little children, with whom I am again in travail until Christ be formed in you" (Galatians chapter 4 verse 19).

An enlightening scriptural account that brings together God's grace and His holiness is when Moses stood with God on Mount Sinai. God passed before Moses proclaiming:

"The Lord, the Lord, a God merciful and gracious, slow to anger and abounding in steadfast love and faithfulness, keeping steadfast love for thousands, forgiving iniquity and transgression and sin, but who will by no means clear the guilty, visiting the iniquity of the fathers upon the children and the children's children, to the third and the fourth generation" (Exodus chapter 34 verses 6-7). To be truthful, this scripture makes uncomfortable reading. We struggle to bring these two seeming extremes together but that is exactly what we need to do to accurately convey God's nature and character – we need to hold in tension God's grace and His holiness. We need to be able to bask in His grace and tremble at the thought of His holiness.

Unbalanced teaching on the grace of God in today's Church has made it nigh on impossible for believers to even contemplate that God might be working in holy anger and judgment through the Covid-19 pandemic. "A God of grace would never act in such a judgmental way" would be the cry of many. I would go as far as to say that the lack of balanced teaching on grace has blinded the eyes of most to considering the spiritual implications of the Covid-19 elephant in the room. This is a serious indictment on the teachers of God's Word – a failure to consistently teach the whole counsel of God whereby God's people would be corrected in their beliefs, trained to live holy lives and fully equipped to understand and face up to whatever God may be doing in any season of His plans and purposes for mankind. The Apostle Paul states in 2 Timothy chapter 3, verses 16-17:

"All Scripture is inspired by God and profitable for teaching, for reproof, for correction, and for training in righteousness, that the man of God may be complete, equipped for every good work."

A Distortion of Grace

CHAPTER 2 – GRAPPLING WITH THE HOLINESS OF GOD

In the last chapter we looked at the problem of common distortions of the Biblical portrayal of God's grace. Being confronted with teaching that unpacks the whole counsel of God introduces us, amongst other things, to His multi-faceted nature and character.

Holiness is one such facet of God's nature and character that is misunderstood by many Christian believers. Just like grace, the holiness of God pervades both the Old and New Testaments. When the Bible refers to the holiness of God it means the total otherness of God's nature, His absolute purity, His complete and consistent separation from and hatred of iniquity and sin. It also implies a requirement for total obedience from those who encounter God in His holiness.

There are three Biblical examples I would like us to consider, two in the Old Testament and one in the New Testament, that clearly demonstrate or imply such an understanding of holiness:

The first passage is found in Exodus chapter 3, where the shepherd Moses encounters God in a distinctly different kind of burning bush in the Sinai desert. As he approaches this unusual spectacle he is audibly instructed to, firstly, not approach any closer, and, secondly, to remove his shoes as he is now standing on holy ground. The soil was no different from what it was like before but the whole scene was transformed by the awesome holiness of the 'I am'. It was not possible for Moses to walk any nearer to the fiery presence of God without being totally consumed, or for him to bring the soil of the day, plastered on the soles of his shoes, into God's holy presence. As God began to address him, Moses hid his face in fear – he couldn't even look at the One who was speaking.

Our response to God, when we encounter His holiness, always has consequences. For all those familiar with this well-known story of Moses and the burning bush it is well known how he came up with almost every excuse possible to get out of the responsibility that God was calling him to. Moses' final request was that God would send someone else to rescue the Israelites from the hand of Pharoah. Less well known is the next incident in Moses' life, as he was at a lodging place on route to Egypt. We read in Exodus chapter 4, verse 24 that the Lord again met with Moses but this time He sought to kill him! Moses was only saved from death when his wife, Zipporah, took a knife and cut off the foreskin of their son and touched Moses' feet with it. Many gospel sermons have rightly drawn parallels here between this incident and the redeeming power of the blood of Jesus. Generally, commentators have suggested that the issue here was Moses' failure to circumcise his son, an act of disobedience against God Himself. However, I want to offer another suggestion that, having encountered the awesome holy presence of God in the wilderness, Moses had dared to try to argue and wriggle out of God's calling – he had not yet understood that an encounter with this holy God demanded total, unquestioning obedience. The result of such stubborn resistance against God was nothing short of a death sentence. Only Zipporah's lightning response brought God's mercy to bear and saved Moses' life. What a lesson learned that Moses never forgot.

Contrast Moses' response to God with that of Abraham as recorded in Genesis chapter 22. God told Abraham to take his child of promise, Isaac, the son born in his old age, and sacrifice him in the land of Moriah. Not once in this passage does Abraham offer any resistance to God's will and command. Even when his dearly loved son was screaming out in fear and confusion, as he was bound on the makeshift altar, Abraham still raised the sacrificial knife ready to strike. It was only God's timely intervention that stopped Abraham killing his son – it had been proven that the fear of a holy God was deeply established within Abraham's heart. Where had such unquestioning obedience to God's commands come from? I would suggest it included Abraham's first-hand knowledge of God's holy judgment being poured out upon the wicked cities of Sodom and Gomorrah, including judgment falling upon Lot's wife. Also, the flood that God sent upon the World, wiping out all mankind, apart from Noah's immediate family, would still have been a major talking point as Noah and Abraham's lives overlapped. Abraham had clearly learnt from personal experience, and from recent history, that a holy God was not someone to ignore, to argue with, or to disobey.

Anyway, whatever interpretation you prefer as regards the incident between God and Moses, the undeniable truth is that a holy God had sought to kill the one He had just called, for an act of rebellion and sin!

The second passage I want us to explore here is found in the book of Isaiah chapter 6. Again, this is another well-known Biblical account that relates Isaiah's encounter with God leading to his commission to 'go' in response to God's call on his life. But I want us to particularly examine the unfolding of God's holiness as revealed in this passage, and to also see the implications for Isaiah as a result of this encounter.

I want to use a little literary licence here to help us better understand the context of this passage. Chapter 6 begins with the phrase "In the year that King Uzziah died". This may not only provide us with a timeframe for Isaiah's life-changing encounter but also a specific reason as to what led him to seek the Lord on this occasion. The details of Uzziah's story unfold in 2 Chronicles chapter 26. Uzziah had been a God-fearing king for most of his reign in Judah. He had followed the ways of the Lord and, as a result, prospered in all that he put his hand to. However, in verse 16 of the passage in question, there is a change in Uzziah – his regal strength and success produced a pride in his heart. On one occasion, despite the protestations of the priests, he entered the Temple to burn incense to the Lord – an activity forbidden except by the Aaronic priests. Immediately, he was struck down with leprosy and remained a leper until the day of his death. As far as we know, this was the only time Uzziah seriously disobeyed the Lord. All this took place during the time that Isaiah was a prophet in Judah.

My suggestion is that the occasion of Isaiah seeking God, outlined in Isaiah chapter 6, which took place shortly after Uzziah's death, was specifically because of Isaiah's offence at what had happened to his king, who had served Judah so well and for so many years. As soon as he began to seek the Lord, Isaiah was transported into God's holy presence where the glory of the Lord blazed forth from His throne, filling the whole temple. Even the heavenly Seraphim, flying above God's throne, needed to cover their faces and feet in the presence of the Lord of hosts, as they proclaimed to each other "Holy, holy, holy is the Lord of hosts; the whole earth is full of His glory." Isaiah's immediate and well-known response was "Woe is me! For I am lost". Suddenly, in the light of God's brilliant purity and righteousness, Isaiah recognised the depravity of his own heart – the murmurings in his heart and the mutterings on his lips, shared by those around him, were totally unclean. The word translated as 'lost' in Isaiah's response to this glorious vision of God, can also mean 'destroyed' or 'ruined'. In common English we could rewrite Isaiah's response as "Crying out in utter despair, Isaiah recognised he was now a dead man!" This prophet of God had been transported to a new level spiritually in the light of the revelation of God in all His holiness – perhaps he recognised for the first time that nothing unclean can ever be present in God's presence – sin always has consequences. Uzziah's sinful actions in God's Temple brought upon him the judgment of being a leper for the rest of his life. Up to this point, this one sin of Uzziah seemed, to Isaiah, to have been harshly punished, but now he understood the dark consequences of even one act of pride and rebellion against a holy God.

The third passage is found in the New Testament, in the book of Revelation, chapter 4. We have here another revelation of God seated on His heavenly throne, where His glory is manifest, this time to the apostle John. This account is not so different to that found in Isaiah chapter 6 – some of the descriptions in Revelation are almost identical to those in Isaiah. The thing that is most striking is the identical response of the heavenly creatures in the trifold proclamation affirming God's holiness: "Holy, holy, holy, is the Lord God Almighty, who was and is and is to come" (verse 8). This is so significant – whilst it is true to acknowledge and affirm the magnitude of God's love, mercy, faithfulness and goodness, none of these attributes are ever proclaimed in the pages of Scripture as in the trifold proclamations of God's holiness, found in both Isaiah and Revelation. Holiness is the first thing we discover about God's nature as He is revealed in the heavenly throne-room. For this reason, I would suggest that holiness is the chief facet of God's nature and character.

So, what can we glean from these passages as we continue to explore the elephant in the room? Is it the possibility that, through the Covid-19 pandemic, God's holy judgment is being poured out today on the nations of the World? If God sought to kill Moses, as he resisted God's call; if God struck down Uzziah with leprosy as a result of his one act of wilful pride and disobedience; if God's prophet, Isaiah, saw himself as a dead man in God's presence as a result of his murmurings of unfairness and discontent, how much more is God entitled to pour out His judgment on the nations of the World as they continually and brazenly act in wilful disobedience against such a holy God?

In the next chapter we shall explore the subject of God's judgment on individuals, families, cities, and nations as it is revealed within the pages of God's Word, again asking the question – 'Has God changed?' Is it possible that we have missed so many acts of God's judgment because of our unwillingness to see God outside the narrow and blinkered lens of His grace?

CHAPTER 3 – IS GOD ACTING IN JUDGMENT?

In this chapter we are tackling the issue at the heart of this book – the possibility of God acting in judgment on the nations of the World through the Covid-19 pandemic. So far, we have looked at the dominance of grace teaching in today's Church which has blinded the eyes of many Christian believers to considering God's judgment in today's World. We have sought to expand understanding on God's nature and character, especially looking at His holiness, which stands, at least as tall, alongside His grace in his dealings with mankind. This is powerfully demonstrated at the cross of Jesus where God's holy judgment and His amazing grace meet like nowhere else in God's Word.

But what about God as Judge? I think many Christians tend to compartmentalise God's judgment – they see it as something that took place in the past, within the pages of the Old Testament; they see it as happening in the future in events leading up to the final judgment on all mankind and on Satan and his angels; however, they struggle to comprehend it in the New Testament era, the time period sandwiched between the Old Testament and the final judgment. Even if they do consider some acts of God's judgment in the pages of the New Testament (excluding the book of Revelation) they fail to apportion any world events to God's judgment from the finalising of the New Testament writings up to the present day. There tends to be an unquestioning consent to the scientific

World as regards the causation of all local, regional, national and even global catastrophes, pandemics, conflicts, etc.

Adding in another point here, even if God is clearly shown as acting in judgment within the pages of the Old Testament, this causes serious theological issues for many, as it goes completely against their understanding of God and how He acts. This has caused many to conclude that, from the times of Jesus' human birth, life, death and resurrection, God has completely changed in His dealings with mankind. However, God hasn't changed one iota in His nature or character – the Alpha and Omega has remained constant – He was, is, and will always be the God of amazing grace, but, equally, He was, is, and will always be an intensely holy Being who demands absolute obedience to His will and ways.

Let's start in the Old Testament. Throughout its thirty-nine books God's judgment is a regular topic presented to the reader – He is seen to judge individuals, families, cities, nations and empires. He uses, as His tools of judgment, floods, famines, earthquakes, droughts, fires, diseases, sickness, plagues and wars. Some of these tools of judgment strike without any involvement of man; with others, God uses individuals, kings and nations to bring about His judgment on cities and nations, including upon Israel itself. Some judgments were immediate, others were for the future. Always God's judgment came as a result of man's rebellion and sin against Him, His Word and His ways. Throughout the Old Testament, prophets were often the ones used to declare the impending judgments of God.

God's judgment on nations is a key feature of most of the Old Testament prophetic books. Often, the nations surrounding Israel are marked out for judgment because of their worship of false gods, their grossly unrighteous behaviour and their actions towards God's people, Israel. In the small book of Amos, chapter 1 opens with a list of tribal nations about to experience God's judgment – Damascus (Syria), Gaza (Philistines), Tyre (Lebanon), Edom (Trans-Jordan) and the Ammonites (also Trans-Jordan). All these nations were bordering Israel. Amos' prophetic proclamations against these various peoples are all phrased in a similar fashion:

"Thus says the Lord: "For three transgressions of Edom, and for four, I will not revoke the punishment; because he pursued his brother [Israel] with the sword, and cast off all pity, and his anger tore perpetually, and he kept his wrath for ever. So I will send a fire upon Teman, and it shall devour the strongholds of Bozrah"" (Amos chapter 1, verses 11-12).

Israel, as a nation, and, as God's people, didn't escape God's judgment either, ultimately being overrun and Jerusalem destroyed by the Babylonians and Assyrians, because of Israel's worship of false gods, their disobedience to God's Word and their rejection of the attempts of the prophets to bring them to repentance:

"Declare in Judah, and proclaim on Jerusalem, and say, "Blow the trumpet through the land; cry aloud and say, 'Assemble, assemble and let us go into the fortified cities!' Raise a standard toward Zion, flee for safety, stay not, for I [God] bring evil from the north, and great destruction" (Jeremiah chapter 4, verses 5-6).

It's important, before we move away from the Old Testament, to take a look at why, when and how God's judgment of the Amorite nation (Northern Syria) took place. In the book of Genesis chapter 15, God revealed His plans for Abraham and the future Israelite nation. After reconfirming His covenant with Abraham, God went on to tell him that his descendants would be enslaved in a foreign country [Egypt] for 400 years, after which they would return to the land of Canaan [Israel]. Included in God's purposes for Abraham's descendants returning to Canaan, was the issue of meting out His judgment on a number of tribal nations within and around Canaan, including the Amorites:

"And they [the descendants of Abraham] shall come back here in the fourth generation; for the iniquity of the Amorites is not yet complete" (verse 16).

So what was so evil about the Amorite nation that invited God's judgment on them and other surrounding tribal nations and why was there a specific delay in that judgment being meted out on the Amorites?

Amongst other things, the Amorites were guilty of the worship of false gods, engaging in gross sexual practices (even within the context of their worship) and offering up children in sacrifice to the god Molech. All this was greatly offensive in the eyes of a holy God. However, God delayed his tool of judgment, the newly established Israelite nation within Canaan, from meting out his destructive punishment for more than 400 years. This highlights two important truths that must be considered when looking at God's judgments. Firstly, God is immensely longsuffering with mankind, often delaying His judgment, thereby allowing time for individuals, families, cities and nations to come to a place of true repentance before Him. This would allow God to extend mercy instead of judgment. Secondly, in God's eyes, there reaches a point where the cup of iniquity, in this case, that of the Amorites, reaches the point of being full or complete. Time for patience has been fully exhausted – now judgment is inevitable.

This reminds me so much of the situation we currently find ourselves in. For so many years, God has been so patient with the nations of the World, and, may I add, especially the Christianised Western nations, but now His patience has finally run out and His judgment is being meted out through, amongst other things, the Covid-19 pandemic. The Western nations are, in many ways, so akin to the Amorite nation – we have rejected the God of Abraham, Isaac and Jacob, the God and Father of our Lord Jesus Christ and replaced Him with so many false 'gods'. We have allowed the worship of other religions to be fully established within our borders, as equal religious practices. We have indulged in every possible variation of immoral sexual practices, including the large-scale systematic trafficking and sexual abuse of women and children. We have far-surpassed any godless Biblical nation in the sacrificial offering up of many children – except we name it the more acceptable term – the abortion of foetuses! But our cup of iniquity has now reached the brim and is seriously spilling over – God now has no alternative but to pour out His judgment on us. His desire is always to bring about repentance which releases His mercy and the ending of His judgment; but, alas, to no avail, for nations desperately search for any other answer but to look to our God and Creator, for His solution. We will look more at the subject of repentance in the next chapter.

Let's return to looking further into what God's Word has to teach us about His judgments.

We've already dealt with the issue of grace and judgment as revealed in both the Old and New Testaments. But just to reiterate, just as the grace of God richly pervades the pages of the Old Testament, so the judgments of God are plain to see within the pages of the New Testament.

There are a couple of examples I want to refer to in the Gospel of Luke and the Acts of the Apostles before turning our attention to the final book of the Bible – John's Revelation.

In Luke chapter 21, verses 20-24, Luke records Jesus' prophetic teaching on the future destruction of Jerusalem and the scattering of the Jewish people across all nations of the World. The wider context of Luke 21 is Jesus' teaching of signs that will precede His return and the end of the age, but this short section of just five verses is an insert, looking at a judgment that will far precede Jesus' return. These verses are referring to the year AD70 when the Roman forces under the leadership of the Roman general, Titus, besieged and plundered Jerusalem, destroying both the city and the temple, thereby bringing about the "days of vengeance" (verse 22). God's judgment was poured out on an unrighteous and unbelieving Jewish generation, who had failed so miserably to recognise their Messiah. According to the Jewish historian, Josephus, more than one million inhabitants of Jerusalem died then as a result of violence and famine; another 100,000 were enslaved by the Romans.

In the early chapters of the Acts of the Apostles we read an example of God's judgment being poured out on a couple who were amongst those who professed faith in Jesus. Acts chapter 5 records the account of Ananias and Sapphira who attempted to lie to Peter and to the Holy Spirit about the proceeds from the sale of a piece of land. They were attempting to appear more generous than they intended, secretly keeping back some of the proceeds of the sale. They were under no obligation to give anything from the sale, but it was the issue of blatantly lying that brought down God's wrath upon them. Firstly,

Ananias, and close behind him, his wife, Sapphira, were addressed with Peter's razor-sharp words of knowledge leading to them both dropping down dead at his feet. Luke records that this incident brought "great fear upon the whole church, and upon all who heard of these things" (verse 11). The Greek word 'phobos' literally means fear or a sense of terror. God was clearly establishing the fear of the Lord in that nascent Christian community – an understanding of God's most holy nature which cannot tolerate even one unrepented sin. Such an understanding of God's nature, alongside that of His grace, permeates the teachings of the apostolic letters. The Apostle Peter, witness to this shocking incident, reminds his readers in his first letter, chapter 1, verse 16, that God hasn't changed one bit from how the Old Testament scriptures reveal Him. He states:

"You shall be holy, for I am holy", quoting from the book of Leviticus, chapter 11 verse 44.

Let's move on now to take a look at John's Revelation, the very last book of the New Testament. So much of this awesome revelation, given to the Apostle John, is about future events leading up to the return of Jesus and even beyond that, to the final judgment and heaven itself. Our main interest, for the pages of this book, is to demonstrate the ongoing reality of God's judgment, even in, what is often termed, this age of grace.

Whilst the language of much of Revelation is figurative and intensely dramatic, there are enough passages which are blatantly clear and easy to understand as we seek to comprehend God's coming judgment upon a disbelieving and rebellious World. In chapter 8, we read about trumpets heralding the coming judgments of God upon the earth – a third of the Earth and its vegetation is to be burnt up, a third of marine life is going to perish in polluted oceans, a third of fresh water sources are to be poisoned, leading to the death of many, a third of the heavens are going to be unnaturally darkened so that the sun and stars remain hidden from view and so on. In chapter 9, we go on to read that one third of mankind is going to die as a result of three plagues (verse 18). We only need to consider current well-known threats to life on Earth, be they so-called natural disasters or man-intended destructions, to picture what these judgments will mean. Whether or not it is man-made, God will weave these events into His end-times acts of judgment.

In chapter 18, John records the destruction of 'Babylon', not the once great Empire of old, which came under His judgment centuries before the birth of Jesus, but rather a name used to describe an end-times worldwide godless and prideful system of government, trade and commerce. John records that God's judgment will fall upon Babylon in an hour (verse 10) – an unprecedented governmental and financial collapse witnessed and experienced all around the World. Again, is this outcome so unexpected in the current thinking of many social commentators, industrialists and financiers of our own generation?

In Revelation chapter 8, verses 5-7, John records these words, describing the justness of all these planned acts of God's judgment:
"Just art Thou in these Thy judgments, Thou who art and was, O Holy One. For men have shed the blood of saints and prophets, and Thou hast given them blood to drink. It is their due!" And I heard the altar cry, "Yea, Lord God the Almighty, true and just are Thy judgments!"

Moving away from the pages of the Old and New Testaments to the centuries between the Apostolic age and the final days of Revelation – is it so shocking to suggest that God still acts in judgment through both natural and man-inspired wars and catastrophes. Of course, it's not right or helpful to assume that every such event over past centuries up to the present has the judgment of God stamped upon it; equally, to consign past recorded judgments of God to the fables of yore, wondering if those events really did happen as written down, and considering future Biblical judgments as more poetic in expression than would-be historical events, is just as wrong and unhelpful. As Christian believers we cannot but conclude that our God has not changed over the centuries, whether during the era of Biblical writings or the centuries leading up to the current day. Our God is the same - He is as holy as He is gracious and forgiving. His holiness demands judgment on the unrighteous and rebellious, just as His grace releases mercy and forgiveness on the penitent. Our God has suffered the insult of rebellious nations, including our own, for many years – is it so unlikely that God should use a deadly pestilence, such as Covid-19, in judgment, to get the World's and the Church's attention? So what is it that the Lord is looking for from us in the midst of this current judgment?

Is God Acting in Judgment?

CHAPTER 4 – WHAT RESPONSE IS GOD LOOKING FOR?

There are at least three main reasons why God acts in judgment upon mankind:

The first reason is that the holiness of God must always be satisfied. It would be a denial of His nature if God was to act arbitrarily – sometimes in judgment and sometimes in overlooking man's sin and rebellion – in His dealings with us. This may be difficult to comprehend but God cannot ignore even one act of sin committed, whether with knowledge or in ignorance. The cross and resurrection of Jesus are rightly the highpoints in Christian belief but not only because the grace and forgiveness of God was released upon mankind through those events; the cross and resurrection equally mark the satisfying of God's holy anger. The only way for sin to be dealt with was for someone to pay the full redemptive price – the shedding of the precious blood of the spotless Lamb of God was the only possible way for this salvation to be released to all mankind. Try and imagine, for a moment, the horror of a Holy God having no option but to see His only begotten eternal Son endure death to enable His plan of salvation to succeed. The excruciating physical suffering endured by Jesus was minimal in comparison to Him bearing the full weight of His Father's holy judgment being poured out on Him as He became sin for us. No wonder the skies darkened for several hours, the earth quaked,

39

rocks were split in two and even tombs flew open at this World-changing event.

The second reason for God acting in judgment is to punish unrepentant mankind with the hope that it will lead to a change of heart and behaviour in an individual, family, city, tribe or nation, thereby enabling God to release His forgiveness and mercy.

At the dedication of the new temple in Jerusalem that Solomon had built, the king prayed an amazing and lengthy prayer (found in 2 Chronicles chapter 6 verses 12-42). At the heart of this prayer there was a clear recognition of the fact that his people would endure judgments from God as a result of their future sin and rebellion against Him. Solomon goes so far as admitting the inevitability of their sin which would incur God's wrath. These judgments would come in the form of judgment on individual sin, military defeats, captivity in foreign lands, drought, famines, contagious diseases and plagues, crop and insect infestations, and so on. Solomon appeals, on the grounds of repentant hearts, for God's forgiveness, a fresh outpouring of his covenant love, and full restoration in their relationship with God. At this point, fire suddenly fell from heaven, consuming the burnt offering and sacrifices that had been prepared, and God's glory filled the Temple (2 Chronicles chapter 7 verse 1). It is recorded later in chapter 7, that, following this dedicatory prayer and God's fiery response, the

Lord appeared in the night to Solomon and spoke these very well-known words:

"When I shut up the heaven so that there is no rain, or command the locust to devour the land, or send pestilence among My people, if My people who are called by My name humble themselves, and pray and seek My face, and turn from their wicked ways, then I will hear from heaven, and will forgive their sin and heal their land" (2 Chronicles chapter 7 verse 14). This scripture clearly demonstrates to us that God would indeed send judgments upon His people in the future because of their wrongdoings, but, also, that there was a way back through humility, prayer and repentance.

The third reason why God acts in judgment is as a final punishment released on those who have failed to respond to His means of seeking restoration – they have brazenly continued to rebel against Him, totally ignoring the Holy Creator's demands upon them as if He doesn't even exist. This is exactly what happened to the Amorite nation – they had had more than 400 years to come to a place of repentance before God, turning from their gross wickedness and acknowledging God for who He was, and submitting their lives totally to Him as Lord and King. God's patience, extended to them, finally came to an end – their cup of iniquity had become full – and a comprehensive judgment from God was meted out on them by the Israelite nation. The same will apply to the nations of the World shortly before Jesus returns and the same will apply to all those who stand before God on the day of final judgment as they are banished to eternal punishment and separation from God with no hope of a return!

I want us to look in more detail at God's judgment being released in order to bring about repentance, examining exactly what such repentance involves, firstly, for an individual, a married couple or a family, and secondly, for a nation or nations.

There are a number of incidents in God's Word where His threat of judgment is mentioned (to Moses – Exodus chapter 4 verses 24-26) or where His actual judgment is poured out on individuals (to Achan and his family – Joshua chapter 7 verses 10-26 and Ananias and Sapphira – Acts chapter 5 verses 1-10) who have sinned against Him. So, it's important to examine in detail what true repentance might look like in such situations. There has to be an underlying assumption that in each of the above-mentioned examples involving individuals, a married couple and a family, judgment would have been avoided if there had been true repentance in each case.

In brief, if we combine the meanings behind both the Hebrew (Old Testament) and Greek (New Testament) words for repentance, they imply a deep, heartfelt sorrow, regretfulness, a change in thinking and a turning around in lifestyle. We can add to these indicators of true repentance other responses gleaned elsewhere in scripture, including an acknowledgement of the deep offence caused to the Lord (Psalm 51 verse 4), a cry for forgiveness and a clean heart (Psalm 51 verses 2 and 7), a desire to forgive and to restore broken relationships (Colossians chapter 3 verse 13), making restitution, be it financial or of a person's reputation (Luke chapter 19 verse 8), and having no desire to return to the previous fallen, disobedient state (2 Corinthians chapter 7 verse 10). It's clear from the above that true personal repentance is no small thing as we seek to be restored to God's favour.

But what about God's requirements for national repentance as this is what specifically ties in with the theme of this book – if God has sent His judgment on the nations of the World through the Covid-19 pandemic, what response is He looking for from the nations in order to release them from His holy anger and to see them restored to His favour?

During this pandemic (and at other times of national crises) there have been calls from certain Christian quarters to take 2 Chronicles chapter 7 verse 14 as our guide to seeing an end to what is happening. Let me, again, bring the words of that verse to mind:

"When I shut up the heaven so that there is no rain, or command the locust to devour the land, or send pestilence among My people, if My people who are called by My name humble themselves, and pray and seek My face, and turn from their wicked ways, then I will hear from heaven, and will forgive their sin and heal their land".

This scripture has generally been interpreted along the lines that if a number of Christians ("My people") seek the Lord in humility, with prayer and fasting, confessing the sins of their nation and asking for God's forgiveness, then He would answer and release the nation from judgment and restore the land to health and prosperity. But is this what this Scripture actually means, bearing in mind its original context?

The context clearly indicates that God was speaking to Israel as a whole nation, requiring a repentant response from all the people – the King, tribal leaders, the priesthood, and all the people. All the people were 'God's people' (unlike a smallish minority in countries of the World today). There are a number of clear examples of national repentance, led by the king, within the pages of the Old Testament, particularly after a rule of a previous ungodly king.

In the book of 2 Kings, we read the record of several kings of Israel and Judah. Chapters 16 and 17 record the reigns of King Ahaz in Judah, and that of King Hoshea in the northern kingdom of Israel (Israel at this time had split into two separate kingdoms). It's recorded of these two kings that "they did not do what is right / did what was evil in the eyes of the Lord" (2 Kings chapter 16 verse 2 and chapter 17 verse 2). So exactly what had they been doing that offended God so much that it brought His judgment on these neighbouring nations? Ahaz, for example, engaged in the heathen worship that the nations, who had occupied Canaan before the time of the Israelites, practised, participating in and allowing sacrifices and burnt offerings in the former Canaanite high places. This worship was known to involve ritual prostitution and fertility rites in front of the altars to the gods. Ahaz is also recorded as having burnt one of his sons as a sacrifice to Molech. He also sought an ungodly alliance with the king of Assyria. It's clear that what the king allowed and indulged in, the priests obeyed, and the people practised, seeking to mix the worship of Yahweh with that of heathen Canaanite gods. In chapter 17 verses 7 to 18 there is a detailed description of the abominable religious practices going on at that time in Israel which incurred the wrath of the Lord. The result was the residents of the northern kingdom of Israel were cast out of God's sight and taken into captivity to Babylon.

In 2 Kings chapter 18, we then read of the reign of King Hezekiah – a complete turnaround in the kingdom of Judah. It's recorded that Hezekiah "did what was right in the eyes of the Lord". The visible repentance in the kingdom of Judah involved the removal of all the high places used for heathen worship practices and the cutting down of all idols and all other places of worship. Hezekiah even cut up the bronze serpent that Moses had made in the wilderness, which the people had degraded by using it as a focal point offering incense to heathen gods. The testimony of Hezekiah is recorded as follows:
"He trusted in the Lord, the God of Israel; so that there was none like him among all the kings of Judah after him, nor among those who were before him. For he held fast to the Lord; he did not depart from following Him, but kept the commandments

which the Lord commanded Moses. And the Lord was with him; wherever he went forth, he prospered" (verses 5 to 7).

It's clear from these examples that, to avert or to bring an end to God's judgment on a nation at that time, it required repentance from the top down – from the king and other rulers right down through the residents of every town and village. It required a complete turning away from every practice that was offensive to God and a fresh adherence to God's Word and to God's ways.

So, what of the nations today? What would be required to turn away God's judgment at this time? What could have brought the prolonged presence of Covid-19 and other disasters to an end long before the effects of vaccines and other health practices? I believe that it would require, for example, here in the UK, for the Prime Minister and the Government, the Royal family, national Church leaders, local leaders and officials, local populations in every town and village to recognize the offence we have given to a Holy God, to humble ourselves before Him, asking for His forgiveness. It would also involve a willingness to turn our nation back to its Christian roots, to turn away from the practices of other faiths, to repeal all ungodly laws that have been passed, especially in the last five or six decades, including current legislation on abortion and other practices that contravene God's Word. This, I believe, is the true context of 2 Chronicles chapter 7 verse 14 and how it should be applied to modern situations.

So what is the likelihood of this ever happening in our post-Christian, multi-faith, hedonistic and pluralistic society where every shade of gender and sexuality is equally promoted? I would say the answer is 'Very unlikely' verging on 'Impossible'. However, to better understand this conclusion we need to look at the wider context into which the current Covid-19 pandemic fits – this is the subject of the next chapter.

However, before we do this, it would be good to look at whether we, as a nation here in the UK, in the past century, have ever had a national turning to God in a time of crisis and what was the outcome. The purpose is to demonstrate what indeed can happen when a nation, from the top down seeks the Lord afresh for His divine intervention. I make no apologies in quoting extensively from an article entitled, 'Seven National Calls to Prayer in World War II' by Dr. Victor Pearce:

"During the course of the second World War, there were times when our nation faced severe threats from Hitler and his Nazi regime. Of seven separate days of prayer called by King and Parliament in the six years of war, as many as three were held within the first twelve months because the situation was known to be so desperate. In gratitude for deliverance after the war, the government passed a law, making Christian teaching in schools compulsory.

Before calling the nation to the first National Day of Prayer, Winston Churchill said he had, 'Hard and heavy tidings to announce'. The commander of the British Forces, Lt General Sir Frederick Morgan, said there was no way out barring a miracle. That miracle happened after the first Day of Prayer.

The first National Day of Prayer was called for by King George VI on March 27th, 1940. The miracle took place during the week following. Most people have heard how the English Channel was absolutely calm all the days during which thousands of private boats and yachts, including my father-in-law's boat, went to and fro rescuing from the sands of Dunkirk 338,000 men of the British Expeditionary Army, leaving only 12,000 sadly to become prisoners or killed.

That first Day of Prayer was followed up by two more within five months, so within five months we had three national days of prayer, not called by the Church, but called by the King and Parliament. But did the nation respond as a nation? They did! Hardly anybody stayed away. The churches and halls were crammed full and overflows outside were sometimes bigger than the crush inside.

Resulting from the inspiration of the call to prayer, we have the story of 'The Town That Stood Still'. A local greengrocer put forward the idea that every shop should close one morning in July 1940 for an hour of intercession. It received the enthusiastic support of the local Traders' Association so the people of Tunbridge Wells, as never before in their history, put themselves in God's hands.

The second Day of Prayer was on Sunday, August 11th, 1940. This was a national youth call to prayer. The King had called all the young people to pray. I was walking past a large area of tennis courts on the way to church. The tennis courts were deserted except for a perplexed young man holding a tennis racket. He was completely alone.

'Where have they all gone?' he exclaimed.

'They're all in church praying for national deliverance,' I said.

'Why don't you go!'

'I can't believe this! My pals have never gone to church even once in their lives!'

The next National Day of Prayer was only a month later on September 8th, 1940. Calling for another Day of Prayer so soon showed how desperate Parliament knew the situation to be. The answer again was immediate and it was during this period that people in the streets began to see angels in the sky. A more determined Nazi air attack was made by sending five fighter planes to accompany every single bomber during the week following. Yet against all odds, as many as 185 Nazi planes were shot down. It was sad for us padres to see the empty canteen tables of those who did not return, but they had shot down a far greater number than our own losses. In fact Air Chief Marshall Dowding said: 'I will say with absolute conviction that I can trace the intervention of God . . . Humanly speaking victory was impossible!' And that was during the week following our third National Day of Prayer, and the newspapers were not afraid to print that statement by Dowding.

My diary records that the next National Day of Prayer was only six months later. It was called by King and parliament for March 23rd, 1941. The guidance of God must have been evident, for we did not know at the time that this was Hitler's next date for invading Britain.

My notes record the following events, which followed the fourth National Day of Prayer:
1. A great earthquake created waves with terrific gales which blew Nazi ships 80 miles off course.
2. That same week, Yugoslavia which had surrendered to Hitler changed its mind and organised resistance.
3. Ethiopia was liberated from Mussolini, Hitler's co-partner.
4. The British Navy fought the Italian fleet in the Mediterranean. Italy lost many cruisers and destroyers and their newest battleship was badly damaged. There was no damage to the British Navy, and no men were lost.
5. The Ethiopian ports were liberated. Haile Selassie, Ethiopia's Christian Emperor, said when no help was coming, 'Then I put my cause into God's hands'.
6. Hitler changed his plans entirely as a result of the submarine earthquake. He gave up invading Britain, and against all the advice of his generals, he turned his attention eastwards to invade Russia.
This was a turning point in the war. We learned later that Hitler had put off the invasion of Britain four times.

The fifth National Day of Prayer was on September 3rd, 1942. It was the third anniversary of the outbreak of war. The very next day at Palermo in the Mediterranean, the whole Italian fleet was sunk. Very significantly, the next month in the North African desert, the Eighth Army under General Montgomery saved Egypt (and therefore Israel) from being invaded by Hitler's powerful tank commander Rommel.

The sixth National Day of Prayer was held on September 3rd, 1943. It was a weekday, chosen at the time because it was the fourth anniversary of the outbreak of war. Italy surrendered to the allies that very night, and the dictator Mussolini was murdered.
It was Mussolini who had invaded Abyssinia (Ethiopia). Emperor Haile Selassie's prayer had been answered. The Ethiopians were liberated, and Haile Selassie became a popular speaker saying, 'I glory in the Bible'.

In the spring of 1944, the seventh and last Day of Prayer was called by the King. The launching of D-Day was delayed several times by the Supreme Commander G. Eisenhower owing to the terrible weather. At last Eisenhower had to make a final decision or miss it altogether, so on June 5th the Allied Forces launched out across the Channel. Eisenhower reported later: If there was nothing else in my life to prove the existence of an Almighty and Merciful God, the events of the next twenty-four hours did it. The greatest break in a terrible outlay of weather occurred next day and allowed that great invasion to proceed.

You may say to me 'The nation prayed on this last National Day of Prayer but what did the Army do about it?' All officers were called to church services, and all ranks came to pledge themselves to God. 'But how deep did this go,' you may ask, 'knowing the varied types of characters?' I can only quote to you part of the address given by the deputy chaplain-general. He did not merely urge religion. He urged faith in the Lord Jesus Christ. The actual services of dedication were held on the eve of D-Day: The deputy chaplain-general was Canon Llewellyn Hughes. He said:

'It is not enough for an army or a nation to have a vague faith in God. It is not enough for us to rest content that our commanders are godly, and that God's flag is publicly flown. Faith in God is useless until it governs action. What does God want done? We believe in God - as what? As a nonentity, content to be recognised, and then ignored? As a vague power, meaningless, purposeless, inarticulate, and therefore unfit to command a platoon, let alone a world? No. We believe in God who wants, and means to have done, all that Christ embodied, taught, lived out. Let an army and a people learn what God stands for, and then they will know when they are for or against His purpose, and support or oppose with confidence as His commissioned servants. That is where the solid toil of consecration comes in. The character of Christ must be known; His goodness perceived and loved; Himself accepted as Master. No special effort thrown off in an emergency will accomplish that; and there is no short cut'.

My memory of that seventh National Day of Prayer is that the nation did not turn out for prayer in the same overwhelming numbers as on previous occasions. What was the reason? Was it that the fear of defeat had vanished? If so it would be typical of human nature, unfortunately".

(The accounts containing the above excerpts were first published in Miracles & Angels, by Dr Victor Pearce and appear on the website: http://www.crossrhythms.co.uk/articles/life/)

Within a decade of the ending of the second World War, Britain had its first visit by the International Evangelist, Billy Graham. His first visit in 1954 was initially surrounded by great controversy including debates in Parliament as to whether his visit should be allowed, the Archbishop of Canterbury telling him he was not welcome, and no Christian denomination standing with him. Nevertheless, he was undoubtedly God's man for that time - his first crusade, followed by 17 more, resulted in approaching half a million decisions made for Christ. Billy Graham himself testified that, with hindsight, he should have stayed in Great Britain longer in those early days, intimating that revival could have followed if he had. Billy Graham even made a huge impact on Queen Elizabeth II, cementing her personal faith in Christ. On many occasions she has testified to the strength received from her faith in Christ in her role of national Monarch.

Were the successful results following Billy Graham's visits a coincidence, or could it be, even though there had been a falling away of faith in the UK following the second World War, that God was looking down with favour in the light of the nation earnestly seeking Him during those extremely testing days?

CHAPTER 5 – COVID-19 IN AN END-TIMES FRAMEWORK

So, what is the difference today between countries, like the UK, and how things were at the time of the second World War? Certainly, it can be said, in that generation, the UK was much more of a God-fearing nation than it is today. For the King and the Government, with the full backing of the Church, and the general populace, to call for days of prayer in times of national crisis is something which it's hard to believe would ever be possible in our nation today. The same goes for many nations of the World. So many have fallen so far away from God, and it is hardly surprising that the judgment of God has fallen upon them through the Covid-19 pandemic.

However, there is a question that needs to be addressed at this point – Is Covid-19 just another judgment from God on the nations of the World, similar, in many ways, although not as serious in outcome, as the Spanish flu pandemic in 1918-19. This pandemic followed so hard on the heels of World War I. Altogether, around 50 million people died. It's estimated that around one third of the World's population was infected with the virus over those two years. As history records though, that pandemic came and eventually passed with life around the World returning to normal. Is the same going to happen with Covid-19? Certainly, the cry of many, including perhaps the majority of Christian believers, is that such will be the case. Are they right to think like this or are they misguided? Are there any other factors that would suggest that another outcome is on the horizon – that this pandemic will be closely followed by other global disasters, whether natural in occurrence or man-initiated?

The biggest topic on the lips of international scientists and social commentators today would certainly be global warming. Almost daily news articles are declaring that, unless this 'man-made' problem is tackled head on with severe cuts in energy practices, which threaten life on Earth as we know it, then we are all doomed. Whether the problem is man-made or not is still up for debate, but the reality is the same – life on Earth as we know it is certainly under threat. James Lovelock, in his book, *'Gaia, a New Look at Life on Earth'* borders on the conclusion that it might already be too late to redeem an environmental catastrophe.

We can add to the above current issues the serious threats of destructive war as global super-powers again start flexing their muscles after a generation of relative global calm. Daily newspapers are again writing about the threat of global conflict, with the current major sabre-rattling nations being Russia and China.

To the student of the Bible, the factors mentioned above, along with a host of other issues, would clearly suggest that something else is at work here, that we are literally in the end game for our World. The times we are living in are what the New Testament refers to as the End Times, when numerous national and international happenings are converging, clearly indicating that we are rapidly approaching the return of Jesus Christ to this Earth and the final judgment of God upon the nations and systems of this World, whether financial, economic, political or social. If this is the case, then we are unlikely to be returning to any semblance of normality as we've known it. Rather, we are in the waiting game for other global events to happen as part of God's ongoing end-times judgments.

In the New Testament gospels there are a number of passages recording Jesus' teaching on the signs that will precede His return to this Earth. In Matthew chapter 24, for example, we read how Jesus was in Jerusalem with his disciples. They had been in the vicinity of Herod's Temple in Jerusalem and the disciples had pointed out the splendour of the Temple structures. Jesus' response must have taken them all by surprise as He stated that a time was coming when the Temple would be totally destroyed. The disciples obviously found it difficult to comprehend such an outcome and immediately associated such a terrible happening with the end of the age and the return of Jesus. This led to a long discourse when Jesus outlined events that must happen before that time.

In Matthew chapter 24 verses 4-8, Jesus spoke of coming false Messiahs and false prophets, wars and rumours of wars, famines and earthquakes all preceding His return. In the corresponding passage in the Gospel of Luke chapter 21, Luke adds contagious diseases to this list of global catastrophes. Interestingly, Jesus refers to these signs as "the beginning of birth-pains". Many Biblical commentators have concluded that this was much more than an incidental description given to these particular end-times signs. Just as with birth-pains, which, as we know, become more frequent, closer together, and much more intense, as the birth of a baby nears the time of delivery, so with these signs – as Jesus' return nears then we will see an increase in frequency, strength and numbers of these signs occurring. This has been clearly confirmed by scientific graphs showing the rapid increase in events such as flooding, earthquakes, volcanic eruptions over the past 60-70 years. The rug of many sceptics, who would argue that these happenings have always been with us, has been clearly pulled from under them, as we see the clear evidence of these accelerating disasters.

Jesus went on to speak about several other convincing end--times signs that would precede his return but an examination of these falls outside the remit of this book. However, it would be good to state again, at this point, some of the last days judgments mentioned in the Apostle John's Revelation as this concluding book of the New Testament is certainly focused on what is going to take place in the run up to the return of Jesus. In an earlier chapter we mentioned the following acts of God's judgment which are awaiting fulfilment, namely, a third of the

Earth and its vegetation is to be burnt up, a third of marine life is going to perish in polluted oceans, a third of fresh water sources are to be poisoned, leading to the death of many, a third of the heavens are going to be unnaturally darkened so that the sun and stars remain hidden from view, a third of mankind is going to die as a result of three plagues, and the World system of government, trade and commerce is going to collapse in one hour!

All this sounds rather grim, and, certainly, the times ahead will be extremely difficult, but for the Christian believer in Jesus, whilst these will be difficult days, they will also be days of great opportunity as many people will be looking for answers as their normal lives begin to fall apart under the seemingly unending crises they face. For the Christian believer, these, and future days, are also full of great hope. In Luke chapter 21 verse 28 Jesus states:
""Now when these things begin to take place, look up and raise your heads, because your redemption is drawing near".
Christians are amongst those who have read the final chapter - the book of Revelation doesn't end on a note of judgment but rather focuses on God's eternal reign, on the New Jerusalem, on the New Heavens and the New Earth, and on the blessings, once death is banished for good, for all those who truly know Jesus Christ as Saviour and Lord.

CHAPTER 6 – WHERE ARE THE PROPHETS?

In Old Testament times, when nations were facing catastrophes, be they famines, failing crops, locust infestations or military invasions, as a result of impending divine judgments, there were always prophets of God. These men were commissioned and anointed by God to stand before kings and rulers, priests and people, and to declare exactly what God was telling them to speak. God even told them that their work would be unrewarding, mocked, ignored and would be life-threatening. Their main message was often one of God's coming judgment on the nation or nations because of unbelief, rebellion, unrighteousness, syncretism and idolatry. Yet, these prophets were faithful to their calling, disregarding of their own reputation, and fearless in their delivery of God's words. Most often they were not trying to predict the future, but rather they were speaking to the present predicament that nations found themselves in.

In today's church we have to ask the question, in the light of the seeming silence on happenings like Covid-19 and other life-threatening crises – 'Where are the prophets?' Since the early days of the modern Pentecostal Movement and, later still, the Charismatic Movement, the gift of prophecy has been restored somewhat to the belief and practices of many churches. However, the utterances, whilst not to be despised, are often words of encouragement and exhortation, either relating to individuals and families and perhaps, in a wider sense, to local churches. But this is different to the calling of prophets, especially national prophets.

Having taught extensively across Africa over the past 17 years, there are innumerable individuals who are given the title of prophet but, sadly, the title given often doesn't match the person, the character, and the prophet himself often has no transforming message to declare. Often the prophetic messages are shrouded in such mystery, that they lack real clarity and could easily be interpretated in numerous ways by the hearers.

Where are the national prophets in the United Kingdom? Where are those who, without fear and favour, are willing to declare the now word of God to Prime Ministers, Cabinet members, the Houses of Commons and Lords, the Royal family, the Judiciary, the Armed Forces, the Police, business leaders and so on? Undoubtedly, if many high ranking members of the clergy were to raise their heads above their pulpits and speak on issues of righteousness, rather than on issues like the environment and less pressing social issues, their jobs would certainly be on the line. So, is that a good enough reason to remain silent when the nation is in desperate need of God's voice to once again be heard in national high places?

There are prophets whose calling is to address the issues of the Church – we have and have had some of these. There are prophets who reveal to the Church what God is saying about and doing in the World – we certainly need more of these. Thirdly, there are prophets who address those in authority in the World and reveal what God is saying, doing and about to do in their nations – these we desperately need.

However, we do thank God that there are a few Christian organisations who stand up and declare the need for God's laws to be upheld in our land. One such organisation, that I have openly declared to be prophetic, as near as possible to the Old Testament understanding of that word, is Christian Concern. The flag-bearers in that organisation have boldly taken opportunities to speak in the General Synod of the Church of England, to stand up in Law Courts across our land , and to speak on National Media. On many occasions they have been ridiculed, spoken over and often defeated before the Judiciary, but still they press on, holding faithfully to their prophetic calling. Let many more rise up and follow their example.

If ever there was a time when there's a desperate need to see the raising up of the truly prophetic voice, it's today and all the remaining tomorrows until Jesus returns. Today we desperately need to hear a spiritual defining of World and national events from God's perspective, a declaring of reasons for what we see happening all around us. Instead of leaving it to the spiritually unenlightened voices of many scientists, politicians, educators and social commentators, let the prophets stand up and speak!

Where are the Prophets?

CHAPTER 7 – HOW DO WE PRAY?

To end this book I want us to consider just how we should be praying in the midst of this Covid-19 pandemic? Many prayers offered up will have been focusing on the sick, on those suffering with mental health, on the bereaved, on the tireless members of the National Health Service, on the success of the vaccination programme, on children who have missed out on so much education, on the suffering of many trying to maintain businesses and so on. All these prayers are highly commendable and I'm confident that they have touched the heart of God.

Others will have been praying that God will quickly bring this pandemic to an end; or, they will have been trying to take spiritual authority over the spiritual powers of darkness that have been attacking the nations. However, the danger with these last two lines of praying is that we may well find ourselves praying directly against the will of God or assigning something which has God's hand of judgment written all over it to a work of the devil.

This is why it has been so important to seek to address the elephant in the room. If God has been acting in judgment on the nations of the World it would be better to fully understand that fact and to then consider how we should be praying in the midst of the current pandemic.

In the small prophetic book of Habakkuk, we read the following words:
"O Lord, I have heard the report of Thee, and Thy work, O Lord, do I fear. In the midst of the years renew it; in the midst of the years make it known; in wrath remember mercy".

Habakkuk was a prophet and a contemporary of the prophet Jeremiah. He lived in the seventh century BC just before the Chaldean invasion of Judah. A national catastrophe, predicted before his day, was now upon Judah. The small prophetic book of Habakkuk was written with this in mind. Habakkuk acknowledged the justice of God's judgment coming upon Judah for their abominations; but despite this, he pleaded for the mercy of God to be extended to his beloved nation. God's mercy was extended but probably not in the full way that he had desired – Judah was still invaded and many were taken into captivity far away from their beloved land. However, a remnant remained in the land.

In Genesis chapter 18 we have an account where Abraham, had been informed by God that Sodom and Gomorrah were to be destroyed because of their "very grave" sin. He called out for mercy to be shown to those twin cities if there were still righteous people to be found there. God agreed to the withholding of His judgment if that was the case. Sadly, only Lot and his family escaped God's judgment as those wicked cities were totally destroyed.

I want to suggest that the prayer of Habakkuk, pleading for mercy to be shown in the midst of judgment, matched by the example of Abraham, is a way forward in praying for the nations of the World, including our own. Today, the nations fully deserve the judgment of God exacted on them through the Covid-19 pandemic, but our compassionate, forgiving God, whilst unable to compromise and forever halt His holy judgment, is always willing to extend mercy as a result of the pleading prayers of His children.

Another way we can pray at this time is to cry out for the Government, the Prime Minister, the Royal Family and others in our nation, that they might have a fresh revelation of Almighty God, which brings them to their knees in humility and repentance. God will never take away anyone's freedom to make their own decisions for or against Him but, in His great love and mercy, He will do everything possible to make Himself, His plans and His purposes visible and attractive to all who have open and seeking hearts.

Below is a prayer that you may wish to use in the midst of this pandemic and other future judgments of God:

Almighty and Holy God, Lord of both Heaven and Earth,
We want to fully acknowledge You today.
We recognise You to be both holy and yet full of compassion.

How do we Pray?

We acknowledge the sins of our nation before You.
We acknowledge the great offence You have endured for many
generations.
We see your judgment today as being wholly righteous.

As Habakkuk prayed for his nation, so we echo his prayer and
say, 'In Your anger, remember mercy'.
For the sake of those who know and love you in our nation,
Bring us through this time of judgment.
As Habakkuk also prayed, 'Renew' Your plans and purposes for
our nation.

Lord, raise up prophets today who will speak Your words to our
nation without fear or favour.
Give them divine appointments with kings and rulers.
May their words pierce deep into hearts and minds,
to bring about change, to Your glory.

Lord, we cry out for our leaders – the Prime Minster and His
Government, for the Queen and members of the Royal Family,
For the Judiciary, for the leaders in the Armed forces and the
Police, for Business leaders and others:
Grant them a fresh revelation of who You are.
Bring them to their knees in humility and in full repentance
before You.

We ask all this for Your glory and praise.
We ask this in the precious name of your beloved Son, Jesus.
Amen.